How to F

Other titles by the author:

Effective Evangelism
Discovering Your Destiny
Intimacy With God

The Father Heart of God
Father Make Us One
Living on the Devil's Doorstep
Just Off Chicken Street
Nine Worlds to Win

How to Have Victory Over Sin

Floyd McClung, Jr.
with Geoff and Janet Benge

Marshall Pickering

Marshall Morgan and Scott
Marshall Pickering
3 Beggarwood Lane, Basingstoke, Hants RG23 7LP, UK
Copyright © 1988 Floyd McClung
First published in 1988 by Marshall Morgan and Scott
Publications Ltd.
Part of the Marshall Pickering Holdings Group
A subsidiary of the Zondervan Corporation

All rights reserved. No part of this publication may be reproduced, stored in a retrieval system, or transmitted, in any form or by any means, electronic, mechanical, photocopying, recording or otherwise, without the prior permission, in writing, of the publisher.

ISBN: 0 551 01727 9

Text set in Plantin by
Brian Robinson, Buckingham, MK18 1RT
Printed in Great Britain by Cox and Wyman, Reading

Contents

Acknowledgement 7

Ever feel like a failure? 9

Chapter One: Victory over what? 11

Chapter Two: Power to turn away from sin 19

Chapter Three: Putting Jesus first 27

Chapter Four: The ultimate and certain victory 31

Chapter Five: Walking in the light 45

Chapter Six: Don't give any opportunity to the flesh 53

Chapter Seven: The secret to the victorious Christian life 59

Grateful Acknowledgement

I wish to express my indebtness and appreciation to Geoff and Janet Benge who helped write this booklet. Their names should really be on the cover.

Geoff and Janet have been faithful friends and wonderful co-authors. Many of the ideas shared here came through the stimulation of conversations with them in meeting places as varied as Bozeman, Montana and Amsterdam, Holland.

Thank you Geoff and Janet, for your friendship and for standing with me through the development of this booklet. I am very grateful.

Floyd McClung
Amsterdam, Holland

Ever feel like a failure?

I grew up feeling like a spiritual failure.

When I was a teenager we often had altar calls at church, on Sunday nights. These gave an opportunity for people to make a commitment to Jesus Christ, and time after time my friends and I would go forward. We knew we were already saved, but somehow we still felt failures. We were unable to keep all the rules handed down to us. I remember the continual sense of condemnation and failure – I was just never quite good enough. Yet my friends and I didn't want to go back to the world's way of doing things – we were stranded in no man's land! We wanted an 'altar' call that would instantly 'alter' us! Why do so many of us, clinging to our faith, struggle on year after year but never seem to enjoy the victorious Christian life?

Paul tells us, 'There is now no condemnation for those who are in Christ Jesus' (Romans 8:1), and we can 'Die to sin, but live to Christ.' Jesus says that the thief comes only to steal and kill and to destroy; but he came to give us life and that more abundantly (John 10:10). I have come to believe and know from experience that moment by moment we can know that abundant life and know freedom from the power of sin over us. This is not to say that Christians can live their entire lives in a sinless state. But I do believe Christians can come to a place where sin is the exception and not the rule in their lives.

Since those early days as a Christian I have discovered some biblical keys for experiencing victory over sin. These are keys that have liberated my personal walk with the Lord, and have brought freedom and release to the many I have had the privilege of sharing them with. They are simple things, but sometimes the simplest things are the most profound.

Perhaps you struggle with feelings of condemnation and failure. Maybe you feel you're not a 'good' Christian. Perhaps there is one sin that has defeated you for a long time. Regardless of your situation, God's word promises us victory over sin. There is good news: we can live in a continual and close relationship with Jesus Christ, and sin does not have to separate us from him.

Chapter One

Victory over what?

Many Christians have spent years trying to defeat something they little understand! In order to grasp a better understanding of sin we need to examine what sin is not.

Sin is not disobeying an arbitrary set of rules. Sin cannot be defined as disobeying a set of rules and regulations that are not Biblical.

My friend David, full of new-found faith and enthusiasm for the Lord, joined a church and was immediately handed a 170-page rulebook! Covered in it was everything from where he could go, and when, what clothes to wear, how long his hair could be, and even to with whom he could associate Tragically the rulebook dealt with everything except what really mattered – heart attitudes. The implication of the rulebook was that if you followed all the rules you were making it as a Christian. If not, you were out!

I wonder sometimes if Jesus would have kept all those rules? He was in fact very scathing of the Pharisees because they had reduced relationship with

God to a set of detailed and often ridiculous regulations. There are some leaders who unfortunately think the way to make people holy is to load them down with a long list of do's and don'ts. This approach, however, only produces guilt and condemnation. The more rules there are, the greater our sense of failure when we are unable to live up to them all.

Sin is not temptation. Jesus made a clear distinction between temptation and sin. Temptation to sin is not sin, but we often think it is. This is a confusion that plays right into the devil's hands. Satan loves us to believe we've sinned when in fact we have only been tempted.

Jesus was tempted in the wilderness, yet we are told he was without sin. We can conclude from this that temptation is not sin. The temptation Jesus faced did not leave him with feelings of defeat and unworthiness. He was tempted, just as we are, when Satan presented him with thoughts of power, wealth, recognition and taking short cuts to becoming all that God wanted him to be. But he did not bow to those temptations and so did not sin.

If we have nagging feelings of guilt, then we need to ask ourselves, 'Have I sinned? What specifically did I do wrong, and how can I correct it?' Ask God to reveal these things to you. He is committed to help us lead a victorious life, and will show us our sins if we ask him to. If, after you have done this, nothing comes to mind, then quite possibly Satan is attacking you with vague accusations of sin. I believe many Christians have confused temptation with sin and so are feeling a false condemnation which leaves them powerless and joyless. If you are feeling like this, go to a mature Christian and pray it through.

When the Holy Spirit convicts us of sin it will be clear what we have done wrong. Condemnation is often vague and related to a general sense of failure rather than a specific sin. False feelings based on the accusation of the enemy can destroy us, but when the Holy Spirit convicts those who are open to him, the conviction will be accompanied by a realization of God's grace and the hope that belongs to those who belong to Jesus Christ. The purpose of guilt is to show us that we have done wrong and to bring us to Jesus! That is what any feeling of guilt should do for you if it is based on sins we have committed.

Paul tells us to resist the devil (and his temptations), and he will flee from us. It is when we entertain temptation and allow it to grow in our mind that sin is produced. If we are tempted and are actively resisting it, then we are not sinning. However, if we welcome it, entertain it and give in to it, then we have entered into sin.

Sin is not a product of our environment and beyond our control. Many people believe certain sins are beyond their control and justify it with excuses such as, 'I hate men. My father raped me when I was twelve', or 'all I heard was negativity when I was growing up. Don't tell me I should encourage my wife – it's just not the way that I was brought up.' These are situations that often occur, but they are not an excuse for sin.

I have heard some people say that the 'devil made

them do it'. They blame their actions on the devil as if they had no choice in the matter. Remember, neither the enemy nor sin can tempt us in a way that we cannot overcome. The Bible promises that with every temptation the Lord will make a way of escape (1 Corinthians 10:13). Don't focus on the sin or the tempter, but on the way of escape!

In the Old Testament God made it clear to the Jews that they could not blame others for their sin. Instead, they were to take responsibility for their own thoughts and actions: 'The word of the Lord came to me saying, What do you mean by using this proverb concerning the land of Israel saying, The fathers have eaten the sour grapes, But the children's teeth are set on edge? As I live, declares the Lord God, you are surely not going to use it in Israel anymore. Behold, all souls are mine; the soul of the father as well as the soul of the son is mine. The soul who sins shall die' (Ezekiel 18:1-4). God will hold the person who sins responsible for their sin and will allow none of our excuses for sin.

God has not only given us commandments to keep, but he has given us the power to obey them. He makes that clear in his words to Cain after the fall in Genesis 4:6 where it says, 'The Lord said to Cain, "Why are you angry and why has your countenance fallen? If you do well, will you not be accepted? If you do not do well, sin is couching at the door; its desire is for you, but you must master it".'

Sin and emotional pain

Being emotionally hurt by a friend or family member is not a sin. However, we must be aware that a hurt can easily become an occasion to sin. It is like a crack in a dam. If it is left unchecked it will cause the whole dam to collapse. When somebody hurts us deeply we can either respond in hatred and bitterness and develop a critical, divisive spirit or we can ask God to fill us with his love and not allow bitterness and an unclean spirit to develop in our heart.

Jesus told us to bless those who curse us. If we don't consciously make this effort and bring the Holy Spirit into the situation, then the wrong done to us will produce a harvest of sin in our life. We are responsible for our reactions to hurt that occurs in our life. It is our choice, and God will hold us accountable.

Sin always produces hurt, always robs us of the joy of close fellowship, whether that is with our heavenly Father or with our family and friends. Sin does not occur in a vacuum, but widens out to affect the lives of many others.

Sin is more than outward action. Jesus talked much about sin, and more often in the context of inward attitudes than outward actions. He said, 'Not what enters into the mouth defiles the man, but what proceeds out of the mouth, this defiles the man . . . But the things that proceed out of the mouth come from the heart, and those defile the man' (Matthew 15:11,18). We often focus on outward sins – sins of commission – but there are also sins of the heart, secret sins, secret thoughts. Jesus contended that if a person plots a sin but does not carry it out in action, he is just as guilty as if he had committed the act. If, for example, a businessman plans to commit adultery with his secretary but on the way to the hotel she has an accident and can't make the rendezvous, in his heart he is guilty of the sin of adultery, even though he did not physically commit that sin.

God's holding us accountable for the intent of our heart stands in stark contrast to the world's system. Imagine someone being brought to court for privately contemplating stealing the petty cash box from their employer. It could not be done, because men cannot read other men's minds and know what they are thinking. However, God can read our minds! 'Man looks at the outward appearance, but the Lord looks at the heart' (1 Samuel 16:7). Moreover, Jesus promises that the things we think in private will one day be shouted from the rooftops!

From examining what sin is not we gain a clearer picture of what it is. It is deliberate violation, either by thought or action, of what we know to be right and true in our heart and conscience. Sin is breaking God's moral laws. It is giving in to temptation when, at the root of our being, we know it is wrong and will ultimately bring pain to ourselves and others. It is rebellion against God, for by willingly committing sin we are saying to God, 'I know it's wrong and you don't approve of it, but I want it!' Our sin brings heartache and pain to mankind and to the God of love who created us for himself.

Throughout Christian history there has been much

debate as to whether we, as humans, *have* to sin. Is there a genetic reason for sin, or is it strictly a choice each individual makes? In the personal context this argument is beside the point, and instead we should be asking, 'Have I sinned?' If so, let's deal with the reality of our failure and not get into a long theological controversey about why people sin. The fact of the matter is that we all do sin. The Bible says very simply, 'all have sinned and fall short of the glory of God' (Romans 3:23). I belive every man has ratified Adam's rebellion. Man has become by nature a sinful creature. What is important is that we accept responsibility for our sinfulness and not blame it on others.

Despite the seeming hopelessness of man's universal selfishness, there is hope. God has not abandoned us to sin, but has provided a wonderful means of reconciliation and forgiveness – his Son, Jesus. Through the atoning death and subsequent resurrection of Jesus Christ, we can be set wonderfully free, no longer enslaved to the power of sin. This is not to say that we will always be free from the enticement of sin, but it provides us with the means of winning the struggle with sin and entering into the victorious Christian life. The principles set out in the remainder of this book are weapons that each one of us can employ in that ongoing struggle.

Chapter Two

Power to turn away from sin

Repentance. Is it merely a feeling of remorse that sweeps over us, or wishing we hadn't done something that backfired on us? When do we know we have truly repented?

We are told in 2 Corinthians 7:10 about a 'godly sorrow' and a 'worldly sorrow'. Godly sorrow is repentance, worldly sorrow is regret. Repentance infers that if we had the opportunity to commit that sin again we would not. Regret, on the other hand, implies that we would do it again, but in such a way as to avoid the consequences. I'm sure 90 per cent of the prisoners in jails regret committing the crime that led to their imprisonment, and given the chance again would not commit *that* crime again. Yet many prisoners spend months, even years, plotting the 'perfect crime'. They have no intention of giving up their criminal lifestyle – they only want to avoid the consequences.

As another example take the unmarried girl who gets pregnant. She may either regret not taking proper precautions, or repent of having had sex outside of marriage. Repentance means that we see the intrinsic wrong of our sin. The outworking of this is that when confronted with the same temptation another time we want to say 'No'. Regret is only sorrow about not covering our tracks.

True repentance occurs when we begin to see sin from God's point of view – when we see the way our sin has broken his heart. Perhaps the idea that God's heart can be broken by our sin is new to you. In Genesis 6:5-6 we are told, 'Then the Lord saw that the wickedness of man was great on the earth, and that every intent of the thoughts of his heart was only evil continually. And the Lord was sorry that he had made man on the earth, and he was grieved in his heart.' God was so disappointed with what he saw that there was a grief or sorrow in his heart.

Jesus also was brokenhearted as he wept over Jerusalem. 'O Jerusalem, Jerusalem, the city that kills the prophets and stones those sent to her! How often I wanted to gather your children together, just as a hen gathers her brood under her wings, and you would not have it!' (Luke 13-34). God's heart aches over our sin. It alienates us from him and from our fellow believers.

The greatest motivation for repentance

If we want to have victory over sin, then we must see our sin from God's perspective. Experiencing the sorrow God feels over sin will touch us in a way nothing else can. No sermon on hell can ever change a person's heart like seeing the grief sin has brought to the heart of the one who created us. We must ask God to show us what our sin does to him. *As we do this and begin to understand his great love for us despite how much we have hurt him and grieved his heart, then turning away from that sin is the natural thing to do.* This is the test of our sincerity and of the level of our desperation to be right with God. The Holy Spirit is continually at work in our hearts to help us respond in this manner. Paul says in Romans 2:4, 'do you show contempt for the riches of his kindness, tolerance and patience, not realizing that God's kindness leads you toward repentance?'

I remember how hurt I was when I realized my daughter Misha, who was six years old at the time, was lying to me. My wife Sally and I had read in several child-rearing books that children often go through stages like this and they suggested we demonstrate to our child the importance of telling the truth. We tried every way we could think of to do this. We discussed it with her, spanked her, took away privileges and encouraged her when she told the truth. But all was to no avail. Her lying got worse. Eventually, out of desperation, we stopped everything and started to pray. (Parents as well as children can be slow learners!)

One morning soon after that I felt the Lord say, 'Take Misha for a walk before she goes off to school.' When we had walked some distance from the house I stopped and knelt down so I could look her in the eyes. Very gently I said, 'Misha, I just can't trust you any more.' Tears began to roll down my cheeks as I continued, 'It hurts daddy so much that he can't trust his daughter. What are we going to do about it?' She was taken by surprise at my tears. She had seen us threaten, spank and reprimand, but never cry over the situation. Her little face grimaced in sorrow and I could see that for the first time she understood that her sin was affecting me and our relationship. I didn't say anymore and we arranged to meet in my office after school.

Sally and I were waiting for her in my office when she arrived home from school. I repeated the question, 'Misha, what are we going to do?' She walked over to me and began to cry. 'Daddy, what can I do so you will trust me again?' She threw her arms around me and sobbed, 'Daddy, I'm sorry. Please forgive me. I don't want to hurt you.' Sally and I began to weep with her and I said, 'Misha, we forgive you'. After I had said those words something changed in the situation. Trust for Misha returned to my heart. That was not the first time she had apologized for lying to me, but I knew that this time she had had a revelation of how much her sin hurt me. In her six-year-old heart she truly repented that day. I forgave her, and trust was restored. From that time on the pattern of lying in her life was broken.

I want to challenge you to be very serious with God at this point. It is absolutely essential to set aside time with God – at least an afternoon or evening – where you can ask him to show you your heart from his perspective. A prayer like the one below can be a good starting point:

Dear Lord Jesus,

I cannot see or fully understand my heart's motives. I desperately need you to give me a revelation of my heart as you see it. I ask you, Lord Jesus, to come by your Holy Spirit and show me those things in my heart that grieve and displease you. Show me any root of pride or independence, and show me the manifestations of my sinful nature. Show me my heart as you see it. I need to see how it hurts you and others.

Protect me from condemnation and introspection. I ask that this will be a work of your Spirit, and not just myself looking inward. May I see your character, your holiness and your greatness.

Show me your love for me as an expression of your holiness and how you long for me to do nothing that would grieve you.

Thank you that you died on the cross to set me free from sin, and that you are praying and interceding for me to live the kind of life that will please you. In Jesus' name I pray.

Amen.

I remember Don, the youth leader in a church my father pastored. He set aside several days to pray and ask God to reveal how he viewed his heart. At eleven o'clock on the second night there was a loud thump on our door and my father got up to answer it. At the door he found Don weeping. 'Pastor McClung, please pray with me,' he said. 'God has shown me how ugly my heart is!' My father spent a long time praying with him that night. As a result, over the next months Don's whole outlook on life changed. He began caring so much more about others and had a zeal to win the lost. It was obvious to us all that Don had not merely spent his time in personal contemplation and introspection – he had truly met with God.

Each of us needs to see our sin from God's viewpoint, but we also need to go on and claim the victory and joy he has for us as we overcome. To stay in a state of conviction by the revelation of our hearts is to miss the whole purpose of that revelation – that of repentance and entering into victorious Christian living. After God has shown you his grief and sorrow over sin, ask him for his forgiveness and receive it by faith, purposing in your heart to turn away from those things that have grieved the Lord.

And if you sin again, come back to the Lord again. If the thought comes into your mind, 'You have failed, you can never make it, you are nothing but a hypocrite,' agree in principle! But do not accept the lie that there is no hope. Each time you fail, come back to the Lord. *Let your weakness drive you back to the Lord Jesus, so that a whole new level of dependence on the Lord grows in your heart.*

The enemy wants to use our failures to keep us away from the Lord, but don't give in to his lies. I find it helpful to say to the enemy or myself or whoever says I've blown it, 'You're right, and I accept responsibility for it. I've failed again, but I bring it to Jesus. Lord, I'm sorry. Please forgive me. This really discourages me, but I refuse to let this come between you and me, Lord. I choose to be sincere even though I feel like a terrible failure. You are the only one who can really help me and forgive me, Lord. I receive your forgiveness because of the promise in your word to forgive me any time I come to you and confess my sin. Thank you, Lord Jesus.'

The promise of forgiveness is found in 1 John 1:9: 'If we confess our sins, he is faithful and just and will forgive us our sins and purify us from all unrighteousness.' I suggest you memorize this verse right now if you have not done so already.

The fruit of repentance

There are times when God may prompt us to go and confess to and ask forgiveness of those we have sinned against. He may also ask us to make restitution to these people. Sometimes it can be confusing to know exactly who to go to, and we must listen closely to the voice of the Spirit. As a general rule, though, we should go to those directly affected by our sin. If it is between you and God, then go to him in prayer. If you have had a poor attitude which has caused tension at work, then go to your boss or to those workmates your attitude has directly affected. If, on the other hand, you have had impure thoughts towards another person and they are unaware of it, then it is a matter between you and God. To go to that person and confess your sin in this instance can often cause unnecessary damage to the person and to your relationship with them.

So true repentance occurs when we see what grief

our sin has brought to God's heart and when we determine that we will not, even if we find ourselves in the same circumstances, commit that sin again. However, our motive for not committing that sin again should not be the pain and grief it will bring *us*, but because of the pain and grief it will bring to God's heart.

Chapter Three

Putting Jesus first

Imagine that my wife's reply to the letter I wrote asking her to marry me had gone something like this:

Dear Floyd,
 I would love to marry you. It's a dream come true. Thank you. There are a few minor details, though. I have a couple of other boyfriends – well, ten to be exact. Most of them don't mean much to me, but can I keep Fred and Dennis? I must be in love – I've never previously been willing to give up so many of my boyfriends! Mom says you're a lucky man! Secondly, 'McClung' – don't you think that's a strange name? I don't know why you put up with it. I would die of embarrassment if I had to use it. My last name is much better, so I'll keep it.
 There's one last thing. I will accept your proposal on the condition that I can stay in Texas and live with my parents. I love them. They have done so much for me that I couldn't dream of leaving them. You wouldn't want me to hurt their

feelings, would you? However, you can visit whenever you want. I'm sure you'll understand. I look forward to setting the wedding date!
Yours in undying love and devotion,
Sally.

If I had received that kind of reply from Sally to my marriage proposal I would not have married her. I don't think any of us would marry a person who responded in that way! When I asked Sally to marry me I expected that she would lay aside all others for me, and I would do likewise. That is what marriage is about – committing ourselves wholeheartedly to the other person. We would feel cheated if our partner suggested any other kind of relationship than this.

How then does God feel when we say, 'Lord I love you so much that I'm going to give up everything in my life except Johnny' – or Suzy, or my stereo, or my car, or my job, or whatever else is important to us? Or, 'I want to serve you, but please don't send me to the mission field. I couldn't do that to my family!'

We're told in James 1:7-8 that, 'a double-minded man is unstable in all his ways.' Double-mindedness leads to frustration and undermines the power God wants to give us. God longs to pour his Spirit into our lives and give us the motivation and ability to make right choices in life. He doesn't demand a certain level of maturity and intellectual ability, or recognition from our peers before he will do this. All he requires is our unswerving, total commitment to him.

Total commitment seems easy in church on Sunday morning. But putting Jesus first in our lives has to be worked out on a daily basis. It has to be lived out in the face of constant pressure to conform to the spirit of this world. This pressure can come from a myriad different sources: from friends, acquaintances, people we work with or go to school with, through the various media. However, Jesus wants to give us the strength to withstand this pressure so that we can live our lives to love and please him.

Paul speaks of this concept: 'Do you not know that if you yield yourselves to any one as obedient slaves, you are slaves of the one you obey, either of sin which leads to death, or of obedience which leads to righteousness?' (Romans 6:16). He asserts that every one of us is a slave to somebody! Some of us are 'love slaves', and some of us are 'sin slaves'. Who do we serve? We cannot serve two masters.

Paul goes on to say, 'But thanks be to God that you who were once slaves of sin, have become obedient from the heart to the standard of teaching to which you were committed' (verse 17). So, though we were once slaves to our passions, desires, fears and hurts, we have now been set free. No longer do we have to be enslaved to those things that once held us prisoner.

You can be free from the power of sin! But there is a price to pay.

Jesus told the parable of a man who went to build a tower but did not have enough money to complete it. He said the man should have sat down and calculated the cost before starting. It would have saved embarrassment and wasted effort. 'So therefore,' Jesus says 'whoever of you does not renounce all that he has cannot be my disciple' (Luke 14:27). Every Christian must pause and count the cost of putting God first in his life. If we are not ready to make that total commitment, then we need to admit to ourselves that we will never enter into and enjoy victorious Christian living.

There are accounts of the great American evangelist Charles Finney refusing to pray with people for salvation. At times people begged him to pray, but he refused, saying they needed more time to repent before God and consider the seriousness of their conversion. This may seem harsh by today's standards, but as a result Finney had a very high rate of converts who zealously lived for Christ all their lives. This happened because he did all that was possible to ensure their full repentance first. I wonder sometimes if much of the 'backsliding' we hear of today happens because we have eased people into a 'non-repentance, non-relinquishment' type of conversion.

Chapter Four

The ultimate and certain victory

Lord of all – or not of all

Jesus must be Lord of all of our life or he cannot be Lord at all. That does not mean that we must be perfect in order to accept Jesus Christ as our Saviour. Nor does it mean that we must live the rest of our life sinlessly and it does not mean that we will not struggle to give some things up to the Lord. For example, most of us are emotionally attached to certain things in our life: food, friends, job, or lifestyle. These things give us a feeling of security, identity, and meaning. It takes time for revelation from the Holy Spirit to penetrate our hearts and for us to realize our identity and security must be in the Lord. Making Jesus Lord does not mean that there will not be a struggle in the process of putting the Lord first. It does mean that to the best of our knowledge we will submit everything in our life to him and that we seek him as our source of security and not people or things. It means that we will dedicate ourselves 100 per cent to live for the Lord Jesus Christ, to the best of our understanding.

It also means that we will grow in the knowledge and understanding of what it means to make Jesus the Lord of our life. We will have unfolding understanding of how that applies to different dimensions of our life. We should not be shocked that we need to continue to repent of things in our life that are sinful. Making Jesus the Lord of our life also means there is no intentional holding back. We must place him in our hearts to let him sit on the throne of our heart. He becomes, in effect, a benevolent despot.

It should be pointed out that he is the only one qualified in the universe to hold that place in our hearts! It is because of his character and what he has done on the cross that he has earned the right to rule our lives so absolutely.

In every person's heart there is a cross and there is a throne. If we are seated upon the thone of our life, then, in effect, Jesus is dead in us. It means we have not invited him to come, in his resurrection power, to rule over us. If we will get down off the throne and we will take the cross (that is we 'die' to the ambition and need to rule over our own lives) and we ask Jesus to take the throne and rule over our hearts, then we have made Jesus the Lord of our lives. (Romans 8:9-17)

There are far too many professing Christians who want all the blessings of being a Christian: forgiveness, healing, hope, eternal life, etc., but they do not want to pay the price of dying to their own will and letting Jesus rule over them. Jesus does not want to break our will, but he will cross it. We must subjugate our will to his. We must put his will above our will. In that process, we must die to ourselves in the sense that we will not insist on living for what we want first, but put his character and his will above our own.

If we seek to bargain with God, we will destroy the heart of the gospel and it will lose its effectiveness in our lives. There can be no compromise when it comes to making Jesus the Lord of our lives. Either he is the Lord of all or not at all. He wants to be King over every dimension of our life: friends, family, job, economic security, future plans, hobbies, recreation, lifestyle, living situations. Everything is to be put under his lordship.

You might say, 'Well, I'm doing pretty good. I have given most of those areas to the Lord, I am holding back on just one or two'. I don't want to shock you, but that is not enough. Jesus does not want 51 per cent or even 98 per cent control of our lives. He wants to be in control of all areas.

Picture your life like the chart below:

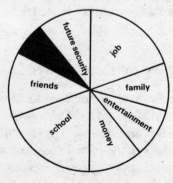

You might say, 'I have given God everything except . . .'. Is there one area that you have still held back from him? If so, you are telling God what part of our heart he can have. Even if we have given him control over 90 per cent of our life, what we are really saying is that *we* are sitting on the throne of our heart and we are telling God what part of our life is his! That will never do.

If we are bargaining with God or trying to negotiate with him, then we have not yet comprehended what it means to be a real Christian. One of the great reasons why professing Christians do not have victory over sin is because they try to bargain with the creator of the universe.

My friend, he does not want 51 per cent, nor does he want 98 per cent but he wants all of your life.

It is possible for us to call ourselves Christians, do good things for Jesus and die and go to hell. The Bible says in Matthew 7:21,

> Not everyone who says to me, 'Lord, Lord' shall enter the kingdom of heaven, but he who does the will of my Father who is in heaven.

Don't try to go two ways at once

Not only is it an insult to the creator of the universe to give him anything less than absolute control over our lives, but it is also insane. The most foolish thing a human can do is refuse the all-wise, infinitely loving, absolutely pure, holy, just, forgiving, merciful, creator of the universe and his rightful place over our lives as his creation.

Imagine a person being at a party and a friend comes and says that they would like to take them out for a drink afterwards. He has been thinking for some time that he would like to spend time with his friend so he accepts the invitation. He says, 'I will meet you outside after the party is over.'

Another friend sees him a little while later and says, 'I'd love to take you and show you my new apartment.' He thinks, 'I would love to see his new apartment, why not? I'll do it.' So he says, 'Yes, I will meet you outside after the party and go with you.' After the party is over, he makes his way outside and his two friends are waiting. Both have their cars sitting side-by-side headed in opposite directions. He wants to go with both of them so he puts one foot inside one car and another foot inside the other car and says to both friends, 'Let's go!'

Both friends take off at once and our friend finds himself splattered on the ground. Psychologists have a term for this. They call it 'frustration'. They define frustration as having opposing goals. I would like to say to you that anybody that tries to live supremely for himself and for God, who tries to go two different ways spiritually at the same time, will be a frustrated person! There can be no victory in the Christian life if we are living for ourselves and trying to live for the Lord at the same time. We must make Jesus Lord of all.

Again, I want to stress that this does not mean that our life will be sinless or that we will live in some state of absolute perfection. What it means is that to the best of our knowledge, and this knowledge will grow as God gives us more understanding through teaching and the study of his Word, of what he expects and requires of us. As he increases our understanding of what it means to make him Lord, then at each new stage of our life we must invite him afresh and anew to be Lord over our lives. The relationship we have with the Lord should be dynamic and growing. His Lordship is ever-expanding and increasing so that we know more and more what it means to invite him to rule over our lives.

Making Jesus Christ the Lord of all also means that we must be doing this from motives that are free from selfishness. We make choices on different levels, in fact there are three basic kinds of choices that every person makes.

1 Routine choices. These are the normal everyday decisions we make in business, family, and school. These affect from what colour clothes we should wear to what we eat to what newspaper we read.
2 Major choices. These are the choices that have much greater implications for our lives. Who should I marry? Should I move to another city? What college should I go to? We don't make these decisions as often and when we do make them, they have greater impact on us.
3 The ultimate choice. This choice can be made more than once, but it is only made about one thing. That is whether or not we will live for God.

It is possible to make routine and major choices for God, but on the ultimate level to continue to live for ourselves. We should picture that in the following way:

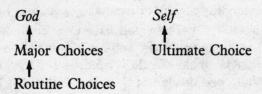

We can make decision to go to church, to be church members, to give money, to sing in the choir, or to do other wonderful and important things for God; however, if our ultimate motive is to do them for self-gratification, to impress other people, or to do these things for selfish motives, then what we have is a well-refined state of hypocrisy. The result is doing good works, the kind of people described in Matthew Chapter 7, but people who are not ultimately living for God. That is why it is so important to make Jesus our Lord from a motive to please him and not to get something from him. We must give him our business, our family, our relationships, in order to please him, to bring joy to his heart.

The motivation for making Jesus the Lord of our life should not be to get ourselves into heaven, to impress God with our spirituality, or to try to get God to love us. Jesus wants us to choose him as Lord because we understand who his is, what he has done for us on the cross, and how we can never live our lives without him. He wants us to make this choice out of a selfless motive of pleasing him and not only for what we can get from it.

As you have read through this chapter, has it become apparent to you that there are things that you have held back from the Lord Jesus? Are there dimensions of your life that you have not put under his Lordship? Perhaps you have even come to the startling discovery, which some professing Christians do, that all their life they have been doing their religious good deeds but their motivation has been overwhelmingly selfish. If you have made that kind of discovery as you have read this chapter, there is only one adequate response. I encourage you to bow before the Lord Jesus, confess your need of him, ask him to forgive you for your selfishness, and choose to make him the Lord of your life. Receive by faith the forgiveness of your sins. You may want to take time to think through what this means. When you do make the choice, please do so knowing that the Lord Jesus loves you deeply and only wants to do what is best for your life. His desire to rule over your life is motivated by his love for you and his commitment to share a relationship with you that liberates you to be all he created you to be.

When we put Jesus first in our lives, we unleash the power of the creator of the univese to dwell within us. The resurrected, infinite, all-powerful creator comes to live inside of us! In his coming to dwell within us, he promises to give us ultimate victory over sin!

It is no small thing to invite Jesus to be your Saviour and Lord. You and I, as creatures, are acknowledging that we are made by the creator. We are inviting the almighty God to take up residence within our hearts. When this happens, he commits himself to us. Not only are we committing ourselves to him, but he is committing himself to us. In making that commitment, he says to us, 'I will guarantee your ultimate victory. I will watch over you and go with you. As long as you will submit to me, I will ensure your victory over sin and your eternal fellowship with me'.

The greatest motivation to victory in the Christian life is this assurance that Jesus is within us and his grace is greater than any temptation we will ever face. He is more committed to our victory over sin than we are!

In Romans 8:31-39 the following words appear:

What then shall we say in response to this? If God is for us, who can be against us? He who did not spare his own Son, but gave him up for us all – how will he not also, along with him, graciously give us all things? Who will bring any charge against those whom God has chosen? It is God who justifies. Who is he that condemns? Christ Jesus who died – more than that – who was raised to life, is at the right hand of God and is also interceding for us. Who shall separate us from the love of Christ? Shall trouble or hardship or persecution or famine or nakedness or danger or sword? As it is written: 'For your sake we face death all day long; we are considered as sheep to be slaughtered'. No, in all these things we are more than conquerors through him who loved us. For I am convinced that neither death nor life, neither angels nor demons, neither the present nor the future, not any powers, neither height nor depth, nor anything else in all creation, will be able to separate us from the Love of God that is in Christ Jesus our Lord.

I can remember talking with Corrie ten Boom about this passage of scripture. She especially stressed to me the truth of verse 37. I can remember her looking at me and saying, 'Floyd, the phrase "in all these things" means just what it says. That is the scope of our victory.' I was so deeply moved when I understood that God promises us that we will be *more* than a conqueror in *everything* we face in life. Everything means everything. All things means all things. That is his promise to us.

What is the source of this victory? It is 'through him who loved us.' We are not talking about some kind of a self-power, positive thinking, pull-yourself-up-by-your boot-straps kind of Christianity. What we are saying here is that Jesus Christ is the source of our victory over sin. He promises us that we will not only be victorious, but more than victorious.

That does not mean that we will not face problems. In fact, it says, *in* all these things, not above these things, or outside of these things. In other words, we will face tribulation, distress, persecution, stress, peril, sword, death, principalities, and powers. But, as we yield our lives to the Lordship of Christ, then he will give us the victory.

It also says in Ephesians 1:4

> He chose us in him before the foundation of the world, that we should be holy and blameless before him.

It is the will of God for us to be holy and blameless! It is the will of God for us to conquer over sin. Therefore, if we will submit to God, he, by his spirit, will come and help us do what is his will for us.

Paul goes on to say in verse 7 of Chapter one of Ephesians;

> In him we have redemption through his blood, the forgiveness of our trespasses, according to the riches of his grace which he lavished upon us.

A little later he says that he has called us to a hope and a glorious inheritance that includes God's great power and the privilege to be in Christ as he rules over authorities, powers, and dominions. If we will abide in Christ, that is, if we totally submit our life to him to the best of our knowledge, then God will raise us up together with Christ and give us the power to conquer sin. I encourage you, if you doubt this, to read through Ephesians Chapter One and 'pray' each verse out loud. Personalize each verse. Get on your knees, open the Bible, and speak those words. Speak them as promises to you. Say to the Lord, 'Lord, I claim your promise in Ephesians 1:5 that you have "destined *me* in love to be your son through Jesus Christ according to the purpose of your will . . . and that you have redeemed *me* through your blood and given me the forgiveness of my trespasses according to the riches of your grace which you have lavished upon *me*." '

Making the scripture personal to you in this way helps make it real to you. Sometimes it is easy to get in the trap of feeling God is trying to push us down and that Christianity is just a list of 'don'ts'. When you read the words of Paul in Ephesians One, it is clear that God is not against us but for us. He created us and he loves us. He wants the best for us. We need to respond to his love by making Jesus the Lord over all of our life. Receiving Christ as Lord assures us of our victory. Not because of *our* choice to make him Lord, but because *he is Lord*!

Pride can be a major obstacle to our making Jesus Lord and experiencing true repentance. Instead of receiving God's grace freely, it's easy to slip into a pattern of earning that grace. We begin to say things like, 'When I get to the stage of praying for three hours a day, I'll really feel like a good Christian.' But God is not waiting for us to come up to a certain standard in order to love us and help us. He wants us just as we are! He may want us to pray more than we do, but he wants us to start where we are, and not think that by doing more for him he will love us more.

This point is nowhere more clearly illustrated than in a situation which occurred in a church in California several years ago. With the influx of Vietnamese refugees into the United States, the church decided to sponsor a number of families. Asians though, have a very different system of values than do Westerners so some misunderstandings occurred. One of the common misunderstandings was trying to get the refugees to feel they were under no obligation to the Church. Some of them felt such a burden of obligation toward their sponsors that they did not even want to see them. To those not familiar with Asian culture, this was interpreted as ungratefulness. The truth though, was that the refugees realized there was no way they could ever repay the sponsors, and so were too embarrassed to face them. Some went as far as moving out of the area.

How tragic this was. All the sponsors had wanted was to see the refugees happily resettled, and not striving to repay an impossible debt. They had sponsored them out of love to bring them freedom, not make them feel indebted.

I think God often feels like those sponsors when we try and earn the grace and freedom he wants to give us. We can't earn his grace. He wants us to freely accept and appropriate it in our life so that we can daily enjoy Christian living.

As we do that, we are receiving the grace and power of Almighty God to overcome sin in our lives. We are receiving the ultimate and certain victory that is ours through Jesus Christ and his death and resurrection.

Chapter Five

Walking in the light

It was John who wrote, 'If we walk in the light as he himself is in the light, we have fellowship with one another, and the blood of Jesus his Son cleanses us from all sin' (1 John 1:7). Today we sing about walking in the light and the phrase adorns posters, napkin holders and tee-shirts. Yet despite its usage in today's popular Christian culture, I wonder if many of us really know what is meant by 'walking in the light'?

The phrase has a very spiritual sound to it, but also has a very practical, down-to-earth meaning. It means living in a state of honesty, where the thoughts and desires of our hearts are known to both God and others.

Imagine that the angel Gabriel is sent to you on assignment with a special moral polaroid camera. This camera can take pictures of your thought life during the last three months or of any time in your life when there was unconfessed sin. These photographs can then be developed and sold through mail order or at the front door of the church for ten pence a piece.

How would you feel about it?

Before we lapse into depression over this prospect, we need to acknowledge that all of us struggle in our thoughts with anger, disappointment and other negative emotions. It is human to have feelings, and God does not want us to deny those feelings. However, he does want us to be honest with him about them. Walking in the light depends not on whether or not God knows, but whether or not we tell him.

Fred is falsifyng the accounts of the company he works for. His employer realizes this is going on but does not challenge him about it. This does not mean Fred is honest with his employer. Only when Fred confesses his actions is he being honest. Whether his employer knows of his actions is not the issue. Likewise, John tells us, 'If we confess our sins, he is faithful and just, and will forgive our sins and cleanse us from all unrighteousness' (1 John 1:9).

My family and I live in the Red Light District of Amsterdam, where pornography abounds and half-naked prostitutes sit in picture windows trying to lure customers. Occasionally people find the courage to ask me how I cope with all this immorality so blatantly displayed.

As I walk up and down those streets day after day, I have found one of the best ways of keeping my thoughts pure and clean is to remind myself that I am continually in God's presence. It is God who has called me to work in this area. I'm not just an inquisitive tourist peering into windows or trying to catch a glimpse of what lies behind the well-guarded brothel doors. If an unclean thought does come to mind, there are two things I have to do. Firstly, I have to be honest with myself. If I am thinking an unclean thought I need to say to myself, 'Floyd, that is impure and you don't want it'. Secondly, I must bring the thought to Jesus. This act of consciously bringing something into the presence of Jesus is what the Bible calls 'walking in the light'.

There is power in the light. There are no pockets of darkness in a well-lit room. For there to be a pocket of darkness an object must block out the light and cause a shadow. Refusing to admit our sins is one way in which we cast shadows in our spiritual lives, and if we are not careful to remove those shadows by acknowledging our sins we will eventually have more darkness than light in our lives. We need to come into the presence of a holy God and say, 'God, here is a thought. It is ugly and impure, and I need your help. I am struggling with bitterness, hurt, and impure thoughts. Help me Jesus. I don't want this thought.' When we do this with each and every sinful thought we allow Jesus to break into our lives and bring his help and light into the struggle.

I have noticed that when I confess my sins to Jesus he doesn't respond with, 'You did what? I'm so shocked! That's the worst sin I've every heard of!' Ecclesiastes tells us there is nothing new under the sun, and nothing could be more true. Read the Old and New Testaments and you will find any number of sins and failures. But read too of the God who forgives, who picks us up and puts our feet on solid ground. He loves us, and for our ultimate good wants us to be open and honest before him and our fellow believers.

If we humble ourselves, walk in the light and are willing to be known for who we really are, then he is willing and ready to help us. Humility is not a feeling. It has nothing to do with the way we walk down the street or our tone of voice. Humility has to do with being willing to be known for what's going on inside us instead of putting up a front to hide it.

In this process of humility and walking in the light, God will direct us to mature Christians who do not have the same problem we have and whom he wants us to open up to. At times like these, the devil may try to trick us by whispering into our heart such things as, 'I can't tell anybody that—it's too bad!' Or, 'No one will ever talk to me again if they know that about me!' These lies keep us from freedom, and we must not listen to them. There is a false kind of rationalizing that says, 'My sins are under the blood of Jesus, so nobody else needs to know about them.'

That is true in one sense, but it is a half truth without acknowledging our need to confess our sins to one another. Telling other Christians about our sins does not provide for our forgiveness; only the death of Jesus on the cross is sufficient to forgive us our sins. But in confessing our sins to others we walk in the light in such a way that it makes it all the more difficult for the enemy to get the upper hand over us. It also assures us of God's love when others know us completely *and still love and accept us*. This is a manifestation of God's love and grace.

Think of all we would have missed if the Bible only

recorded the good points and triumphs of its characters. How would we understand some of David's psalms if we did not know of his sin with Bathsheba? And knowing of it, how much more the beauty and grace revealed in Psalm 51 can minister to us in times of need.

It's not a sin to struggle! However, it is folly and sometimes sin to struggle alone when through the commitment of other Christians God has provided us with his love for our support.

Struggle can in fact be a blessing! Victory only comes after struggle, and Christian maturity means we come to a place of welcoming struggles as an opportunity for growth. James clearly grasped this point when he wrote, 'Consider it all joy, my brethren, when you encounter various trials' (James 1:2).

In the Garden of Gethsemane Jesus himself struggled with his emotions and eventually won the victory over them. Many of us like to read about Peter because we find ourselves mirrored in his personal struggles. We find ourselves rejoicing at his successes and agonizing over his failures.

There is a tendency for those who have been Christians for some time or who hold positions of spiritual leadership to convey the impression that they are beyond temptation. This is a dangerous situation, both for those who think it and for the younger Christians who may believe them. All of us, regardless of our years or position, are going to face temptation and struggle in our lives. *There is potential for evil in the heart of every person, and only by taking that seriously, being accountable to others and walking in the light with the Lord Jesus can we have victory over sin.*

In the Bible the Christian life is often compared to a human lifespan. First a baby learns to sit, then stand, and finally starts to walk, run and skip. If a child goes on for year after year not learning how to walk, we know something is seriously wrong and corrective action is needed.

Today there are many Christians faking it. They are acting happy and spiritual on the outside, but on the inside they struggle with all manner of issues. They have not learned to walk and run spiritually. It is time to take off the mask and begin experiencing real joy. Real joy is built on the foundation of godly humility and is worth having. If we want victory, it starts with humility. We need to encourage this kind of humility and honesty by recognizing that *true spirituality includes being honest when we are defeated or discouraged*.

In the United States recently there have been some Christian leaders who have not walked in openness and honesty, which has led to some tragic results. In high-profile ministries it is tempting to cover sin, override accountability, and put oneself above the need to be open and honest. Christians can encourage this type of action by treating spiritual leaders as if they are able to do no wrong. In these recent cases it was all suddenly exposed, and the secular media loved it as the sordid facts were slowly uncovered. How different this could have been if those involved had been open and honest. Instead of a 'Christian family matter' being worked out amongst those concerned, the whole American public was treated to a public scandal which brought shame and embarrassment to all Christians. It was tragic and unnecessary. Jesus promises that what we think we can hide will one day be shouted from the rooftops. Let's not be fooled. God's standard is honesty, and he will bless us if we walk in it. It is time we began 'walking in the light'.

Chapter Six

Don't give any opportunity to the flesh

Paul tells us to 'Make no provision for the flesh, to gratify the lusts thereof' (Romans 13:14). Put another way, this means we are not to deliberately put ourselves in a place of temptation, either to prove how strong we are or because we are denying we have a weakness in a particular area of our lives. Whatever our weakness may be, we must be mature enough to admit it to ourselves and others. Christians must flee temptation, not flirt with it. It is not common sense to continually present our areas of weakness with temptation.

I love ice-cream – chocolate-coated ice-cream bars, ice-cream sundaes, ice-cream cakes, ice-cream in a cone or even straight out of the carton! Imagine I were trying to stop eating ice-cream altogether. To impress my wife with my self-control, I ask her to make home-made double-chocoate ice-cream with walnuts and almonds! I ask her to leave several scoops of it in bowls around the house: one beside my bed so I can see it when I go to sleep; another in the bathroom so the smell can tantalize me while I shave. Everywhere I turn I want to see ice-cream! If I open the refrigerator door I want to see a bowl of ice-cream with my name on it there, and all because I want to impress my wife by resisting temptation at every turn!

To carry out such a scheme would be ridiculous! If I don't want to eat ice-cream, then why torture myself by having it constantly before me? If I am proving anything at all it is how foolish I am. Alcoholics Anonymous does not encourage those trying to break free of the bondage of alcohol to sit night after night in bleak, smoke-filled bars to prove they have overcome their problem — a devastating result would be inevitable. Areas of weakness in our lives are difficult enough to overcome, without added exposure to temptation.

We have a policy in our mission in Amsterdam. We ask our workers not to witness to prostitutes alone. None of us is above temptation, and we do not want to give any room to it. If we do, it will surely raise its ugly head!

I believe it's common sense that people should not counsel those of the opposite sex alone. Pastors and those with counselling ministries in particular can get tripped up by this. If a pastor is having a difficult time in his marriage and an attractive and vulnerable woman keeps telling him he is the most sensitive person she has ever shared with and that he is wise and understanding, he has placed himself in a position of weakness. Many are able to stand against this subtle temptation, but others give in with devastating consequences. Do not make any opportunity for the flesh.

We must be careful, though, not to shy away from the opportunities God brings our way. If a woman comes to a pastor's office in deep distress and pours out her heart, he shouldn't feel he has to stop her in mid-sentence and arrange a meeting for next week when his wife will be around. The wisest thing for the pastor or counsellor to do is to open the door to his office, ask his secretary or someone else to join him or sit in an open place where everyone can see them. He could then listen to the woman's immediate problems and afterwards invite her over to speak with his wife and himself. The point is not to refuse to deal with the woman and her problem, but to look for ways to avoid temptation while helping her.

If someone has a problem with gossip and spends hours with others who also love to gossip, he or she needs to find some new friends who aren't so inclined. We need to plan things to do when we are with others so there won't be long lulls in the conversation that we fill with other people's business.

If our weakness is getting too physically involved on dates, then why continue being alone together in the car night after night? Why do we always plan dates that don't involve others? All too often we wait until sin is right within our reach before seeing whether we have the self-control to avoid it.

Recently I spoke with Kevin, a young man who told me he thanked God he didn't have any problems with sexual temptation, and that he was completely free from it. I told Kevin he was on very dangerous ground. There is no human being alive who is free from ever being tempted. The Bible says, 'Let him who stands beware lest he falls.' And it is true. We are all capable of being tempted and falling, and failure to admit that means we are not properly guarding our steps. We must be honest. If we have a weakness, then we should not put ourselves in positions where we will be tempted to give in to it. If I don't want ice-cream I should not order it and then have to sit staring at it. If I don't want to spend my time slandering others, then I should not develop close relationships with those who habitually do so.

On occasion I have to walk through the Red Light District alone. I don't like doing this, but there are times when it is unavoidable. So I have worked out a route that does not pass any of the prostitutes or sex shops. It takes me a little longer, but I do not want to present my mind with avoidable temptations.

If we are to give no opportunity to the flesh, then why do I live in the Red Light District at all? The answer to this is, if we must be in a place where temptation is strong, then we should only be there at God's direction and in his strength. Occasionally all of us will find ourselves in compromising positions that could present temptation to sin. However, we must make very sure that these situations are not of our instigation or wilful choosing.

There are some people who become very concerned when, after renouncing their sin and walking in the victory Jesus brings, they still feel prone to the sins that formally had power over them. I like to look at it this way. In a desert there are rutted creek beds which are often dry for years at a time. After rain, the water rushes into the ruts of the creek beds and flows along, because over many years it has carved out those ruts.

Our minds are like those creek beds. We get into the habit of thinking and reacting in certain ways. When we totally give ourselves to Christ the driving force to think and do ungodly things is removed. The power that once held us in those habitual ruts has been broken, but the ruts are still there. Those old sin patterns are the ones most likely to trip us up, and are the easiest to fall back into. The good news, however, is that Christ has freed us from the power they once exerted over us. As we grow in Christ, those old ruts will be washed away. But meanwhile, we have to be alert to those sins and never get so sure of ourselves that we begin to believe we could never fall into the same sins again.

To lead righteous lives we all need the power of Christ, but failure to admit we are weak will lead to our not claiming his stength. The victorious Christian life is not meant to be lived on the edge of a steep cliff face, with us clinging on by our fingertips lest we fall. We should live as far from the edge of temptation as we can possibly get!

Chapter Seven

The secret to the victorious Christian life

There is no pat formula that guarantees we will always enjoy the victorious Christian life. In fact, there are no secrets to overcoming sin. Yet over the centuries and still today, people enter into and enjoy that life. God never intended Christians to live constantly in the quagmire of personal struggle with sin. We must recognize, however, that the potential for sin is resident within us, and struggle with sin is one of the chief ways in which we grow and mature in the Christian life.

The apparent paradox here soon dissolves when we understand that it is not only the presence of sin but how we respond to sin that is important. We must bring any known sin to Jesus, realizing that there is no sin and no amount of sin he cannot forgive if we come to him in sincerity. If we continue to struggle on and on with one particular sin and never make any headway, then something is wrong. You may need to seek help from a godly counsellor or a Christian psychologist. There are many such people who love the Lord Jesus and would agree with the principles that are outlined in this booklet. Asking for help is not a sign of weakness but of maturity.

We are told nowhere in Scripture that we will enjoy a sinless Christian life, but that we can enjoy the *victorious* Christian life. To have victory there must be something to be victorious over, and you cannot have the one without the other. If you go through a difficulty with sin and you bring it to the Lord and you gain victory over that sin so that it is no longer dominating you, you are enjoying the victorious Christian life. If, however, you are making no headway in your struggle and are constantly falling back into personal sin, then you need to read this booklet again, praying over the principles in it and asking God for help to put them into practise.

There are no secrets or magic formulas for overcoming sin, but there are biblical principles that need to be obeyed. And there is wonderful provision of victory over sin through the death of the Lord Jesus on the cross. As we accept his victory and abide in it, then we will know his resurrection power in our lives to overcome sin.

Striving after victory over sin can become a hindrance to finding that which we so desperately seek after. We must come to such an assurance of his love for us and of our ultimate triumph because of what he has done for us on the cross, that we rest in him. Paul encouraged Philippian Christians to be 'confident of this, that he who began a good work in you will carry it on to completion until the day of Jesus Christ' (Philippians 1:6). As we rest in faith, actively trusting the Lord Jesus, we enable the Holy Spirit to work deep in our hearts.

Stop struggling, dear Christian friend, and turn to Jesus, for he alone is the victor. He has conquered sin, death, hell, the grave and all the forces of evil. Give all your worries and failures to the dear Lord Jesus. Worship him and receive from him mercy and forgiveness and hope. Rest in his unfailing love.

If your heart condemns you, remember that 'God is greater than your heart'. He is greater. He is greater than any sin. Come to him now and rest in his great love. Indeed we must obey the biblical principles outlined in this booklet. but above all, trust in Jesus. Do not try to do something to atone for your past failures or to try and earn his love. He loves you *because he loves you*. Accept that fact right now; take time even now to accept his love.

Respond to his love, not by trying to earn it, but out of gratitude. Indeed obey him, but let your acts of obedience be love-reponses to his great kindness and mercy.

Dear Father,

Thank you for your wonderful love for me; I can never repay it, Father, But I want to tell you how grateful I am.

Other Marshall Pickering Paperbacks

RICH IN FAITH

Colin Whittaker

Colin Whittaker's persuasive new book is written for ordinary people all of whom have access to faith, a source of pure gold even when miracles and healing seem to happen to other people only.

The author identifies ten specific ways to keep going on the road to faith-riches, starting where faith must always begin—with God himself, the Holy Spirit, the Bible, signs and wonders, evangelism, tongues and finally to eternal life with Christ.

OUR GOD IS GOOD

Yonggi Cho

This new book from Pastor Cho describes the blessings, spiritual and material, that reward the believer. Yonggi Cho presents his understanding of the fullness of salvation, bringing wholeness to God's people.

HEARTS AFLAME
Stories from the Church of Chile

Barbara Bazley

Hearts Aflame is a book suffused with love for the large, sometimes violent country of Chile and joy at the power of the Gospel taking root.

Each chapter is a story in itself, telling of some encounter, episode of friendship that has left its mark on the author's life.

If you wish to receive *regular information* about *new books*, please send your name and address to:

London Bible Warehouse
PO Box 123
Basingstoke
Hants RG23 7NL

Name..

Address..

....

....

....

I am especially interested in:
☐ Biographies
☐ Fiction
☐ Christian living
☐ Issue related books
☐ Academic books
☐ Bible study aids
☐ Children's books
☐ Music
☐ Other subjects